CW00736154

Create Great Spreadsheets

Time-saving books that teach specific skills to busy people, focusing on what really matters; the things that make a difference – the *essentials*. Other books in the series include:

Writing Business E-mails

The Ultimate Business Plan

Writing Good Reports

High-Powered CVs

Responding to Stress

Succeeding at Interviews

Solving Problems

Hiring People

Getting Started on the Internet

Making Meetings Work

Making Great Presentations

Making the Most of Your Time

For full details please send for a free copy of the latest catalogue.

See back cover for address.

The things you need to know to

Create Great Spreadsheets

Jonathan Whelan

ESSENTIALS

Published in 2000 by
How To Books Ltd, 3 Newtec Place,
Magdalen Road, Oxford OX4 1RE, United Kingdom
Tel: (01865) 793806   Fax: (01865) 248780
email: info@howtobooks.co.uk
www.howtobooks.co.uk

British Library Cataloguing in Publication Data.
A catalogue record for this book is available from
the British Library.

Edited by Diana Brueton
Cover design by Shireen Nathoo Design
Produced for How To Books by Deer Park Productions
Typeset by Anneset, Weston-super-Mare, Somerset
Printed and bound by Hillman Printers, Frome, Somerset

NOTE: The material contained in this book is set out in good faith for
general guidance and no liability can be accepted for loss or expense
incurred as a result of relying in particular circumstances on
statements made in the book. Laws and regulations are complex and
liable to change, and readers should check the current position with
the relevant authorities before making personal arrangements.

ESSENTIALS *is an imprint of*
How To Books

Contents

Preface

Spreadsheets often play an important part in the making of business decisions and in the day-to-day running of businesses. Although they are usually associated with the production of financial information such as balance sheets and cash flows, their use extends far beyond the manipulation of numbers for financial purposes. For example, spreadsheets are used as timesheets, to record and analyse events such as sales or purchases, and to maintain stock records and customer records.

One of the reasons that spreadsheets are so popular is that they are relatively easy to produce and they look professional. They can be included in reports and presentations, and spreadsheet applications can often be used to summarise information graphically, for example in the form of graphs or charts.

However, the professional look of spreadsheets can give the impression that they are 'right' even though they may contain mistakes. Even spreadsheets which contain no errors can be misleading if they are the result of a poor design. Although many spreadsheets are only ever used by the people who create them, a good design can help to minimise the risk of errors and misinterpretation and can make it easier to change those spreadsheets in the future.

This book is about understanding the key elements of spreadsheets, developing spreadsheets that are trustworthy and easy to use and so getting the best out of this powerful business tool.

The most commonly used spreadsheet package is Microsoft® Excel® so this book is based on the terminology and features of Excel®. However, many of these features are also available in other spreadsheet packages, for example Lotus® 1-2-3®.

Jonathan Whelan

1 Mastering the Basics

An effective spreadsheet isn't necessarily complex.
Effective ones are built using simple concepts.
By mastering the basics you can produce effective
spreadsheets.

Things you need to know

1 **KNOWING WHEN TO USE A SPREADSHEET PACKAGE**

2 **UNDERSTANDING SPREADSHEET FUNDAMENTALS**

3 **PUTTING THE BASICS TOGETHER**

Spreadsheets can be an extremely cost-effective way of managing information. The ease of use, flexibility and efficiency of spreadsheet packages makes them a popular choice for many business applications. Even simple spreadsheets offer powerful facilities that can be mastered relatively quickly.

The majority of people who create and use spreadsheets use only a fraction of the facilities on offer. Nevertheless, many office applications require little more than the basic facilities (such as adding together a group of numbers) and these applications often fulfil an important function.

Many people create spreadsheets without having had any formal training and they rely on 'trial and error' as part of a steep learning curve to complete their task. In many cases a spreadsheet is created where the use of another package may have been more appropriate (such as the table facilities which are associated with word processor packages). Conversely, a lack of understanding of the strengths of spreadsheet packages can mean that they are not used even though they may be the most appropriate.

Also, many people's first experience of spreadsheets is having to amend ones created by others. An understanding of the basic concepts and facilities offered by spreadsheet packages is essential for building and maintaining long-lasting, robust spreadsheets.

KNOWING WHEN TO USE A SPREADSHEET PACKAGE

The decision to use a spreadsheet package is not always straightforward even though the need to present information in the form of rows and columns may point to using one. Given that many office packages allow you to create tables, it is worth spending a few minutes considering the main options before deciding on a spreadsheet package.

It is not just spreadsheet packages which enable you to work with tables.

In general there are three types of office desk-top packages that can be considered and each has its merits. These are word processors, databases and spreadsheets.

Word processors

Most word processors (such as Microsoft® Word® and Lotus® Word Pro®) allow you to create and manipulate data as tables. For example, you can create tables and apply formulae to them. Microsoft Word, for instance, includes a number of functions, such as SUM, COUNT and ROUND, and the logical functions AND, OR and NOT. However, if you change any of the values that are used by a function, you have to prompt Word to recalculate the result – it will not do it automatically. (Word gives the result of the function as a field which you must update.)

One of the key strengths of a word processor is its formatting capability, and so **this option is preferable if the data requires tricky formatting such as numbered lists or hanging indents**.

Databases

A database is, in effect, a linked set of tables for which you can build up a complex group of relationships.

Database packages such as Microsoft® Access® enable you to add, amend and delete data by using Forms which act as a user interface to the underlying data. You can use powerful Query and Report facilities to retrieve information based on search criteria which you specify. Like spreadsheets, databases have powerful facilities for searching and sorting data. **They are particularly suitable for storing and maintaining large volumes of inter-related data by multiple users**.

However, a disadvantage of desktop database packages is that they can be more difficult to master than, say, word processor or spreadsheet packages. Also, more people are familiar with spreadsheet packages than with database packages. This is an important factor, as it requires a person with the appropriate skills to build and maintain the database, and to provide the reports and queries that are likely to be required. You will need to be confident that the database can be manned throughout its expected life.

Spreadsheets

Spreadsheets are ideal for carrying out complex calculations, sorting and manipulating data and re-using information which appears in other parts of the spreadsheet.

Spreadsheets come with a wide range of industry standard built-in functions. For example:

- mathematical functions

- statistical functions

- financial functions

- logical functions

- engineering functions

- information functions

- text functions

- date and time functions.

If, for example, you change any of the numbers in a sum (using the SUM function), the total is recalculated automatically. Also spreadsheets have powerful facilities for searching and sorting data, and provide useful options for displaying information in the form of graphs and charts.

There may be limitations placed on you by the package that you are considering using. For example, in Excel 2000:

- the maximum number of columns is 256

- the maximum number of rows is 65,536

- the maximum size of a cell is 32,000 characters.

However, **for the vast majority of applications these limits are unlikely to be a problem**.

Another factor to consider is how you intend to use the information contained in the table. If, for example, you want to include it in a word processed document, you can usually either create a table in the document or 'import' the spreadsheet. If you want to include it in a presentation (for example in Microsoft PowerPoint or Lotus Freelance Graphics) you can usually either import a table from a word processed document or a spreadsheet from a spreadsheet package. (There is more about linking to other spreadsheets on page 67.)

UNDERSTANDING SPREADSHEET FUNDAMENTALS

By having a good understanding of the basics of spreadsheets, you can create valuable business tools.

A key feature of spreadsheets is that the information they contain is arranged into columns and rows. This provides a logical ordering of the information and allows each item of information to be referred to uniquely (using a reference to the row and column in which it appears) – see Figure 1.

	A	B	C	D	E
1					
2					
3					
4					
5					
6					
7					

Figure 1

Cells and cell references

Each 'container' of information, or '**cell**', is identified by its column and row co-ordinate. So the top leftmost cell in Figure 1 is 'A1' and the bottom rightmost cell is 'E7'.

Each cell has a '**type**' which can be:

- numerical data – eg 27, -45.8, 1,003)

- text – eg Sales, 4-Oct-00, Jo Bloggs)

- a formula – eg = A3+A5, =AVERAGE(D5,D6), =Today()

- graphics.

One of the key strengths of spreadsheets is their formula capability; any changes to the contents of a cell are automatically reflected in other cells which refer to it (in a formula). See page 37 for more about formulae.

The manner in which cells are displayed on the screen and printed out onto paper can be modified using the '**format cells**' feature. Height, width, font, left-right alignment (justification) and many other features can be modified and most spreadsheet packages provide useful formatting features. There are in-built formats including number, currency, date, percentage and text. So, for example, formatting a cell as a number allows you to specify the number of decimal places to be displayed.

Ranges

It is often useful to refer to a **range** of cells and this is achieved by referencing the first and last cell in the range and separating the references with a colon. Figure 2 shows three ranges, A1:D1, B3:B7 and D4:E7. The range D4:E7 shows that you are not limited to single rows or columns.

Many of the operations that you can apply to a single cell (such as formatting and copying), you can also apply to a range of cells.

	A	B	C	D	E
1					
2					
3					
4					
5					
6					
7					

Figure 2

You can give cells, or ranges of cells, names (such as 'Interest' or 'Scores') and refer to them by those names, for example in formulae. (*How*: From the Menu toolbar choose Insert, Name, Define. Or a quicker way is to select the cell or range and type the name into the box to the left of the formula bar. Use an underscore for spaces in names.)

Formulae and functions

A **formula** is just an expression that has to be evaluated and most spreadsheet packages use a sign to show that a cell contains a formula (eg '=' in Excel and '@' in Lotus 1-2-3).

Examples of formulae:

- =2.57+5   adding together two numbers

- =B11   reference to the contents of another cell (ie make the contents of this cell equal to the contents of cell B11)

- =A2+B19+D12   adding together three cells

- =A1*F11   multiplying two cells

- =A2/D15   dividing one cell by another cell

- =AVERAGE(A1:A4)   calculates the average of the numbers in the range A1:A4.

AVERAGE is an example of a built-in mathematical function. Most spreadsheet packages have a good selection of built-in functions, the most common of which is SUM. As the name suggests, it adds together the contents of all cells in a given range.

- = SUM(A1:A30) will add together the contents of the 30 cells in the range A1:A30.

- = SUM(A1:B30) will add together the contents of the 60 cells in the range A1:B30.

In Figure 3, cells B2 to B5 contain values and cell B7 contains a formula that is the sum of cells B2 to B5. Clicking on cell B7 would show the content as being =SUM(B2:B5).

	A	B	C	D	E
1	Region	Sales (£K)			
2	North	13			
3	South	15			
4	East	19			
5	West	12			
6					
7	Total	59			

Figure 3

In the above example, if you change any of the values in cells B2 to B5, cell B7 is automatically recalculated. **This 'recalculation' capability is one of the key strengths of spreadsheet packages**; it also lies behind the much quoted 'what-if' capability – see Using Goal Seek on page 56.

The recalculation logic of spreadsheets is very sophisticated and will handle the calculated value of one cell being input to the calculation of another in a different part of the spreadsheet. This may happen hundreds of times within a spreadsheet in all manner of sequences. For example, the totals of columns of values may be either above or below or at the side of the columns to which they refer. Additionally the totals may contain cells that are themselves totals or other formulae.

Relative and absolute addressing

One way of describing relative and absolute addressing is to look at the copying of cells, which is a frequent activity when building and changing spreadsheets.

Consider the example shown in Figure 4.

	A	B	C	D	E
1	Quantity	Description	Unit price (£)	Cost(£)	
2	10	Nuts	0.25	2.50	
3	20	Bolts	0.50		
4	50	Washers	0.10		
5					
6					
7					

Figure 4

The formula in cell D2 is =A2*C2

What will happen if you copy this into cell D3? If you were using a word processor package you would get =A2*C2 again, however, this is probably not what you want and the spreadsheet package will typically modify the contents within the copy function so that you get =A3*D3. This is 'relative addressing' – if you copy or insert cells, the spreadsheet package automatically changes the cell references for you. **Relative addressing is another of the key strengths of spreadsheets.**

So, for example, if you make cell D2 the active cell and put your formula in it, you can drag the 'fill handle' – the small square in the bottom right-hand corner of the active cell – to cover cells D3 and D4.

This relative modification of the cell references works for both columns and rows. However, on some occasions you may not want this to happen and you can override the feature. (*How*: Use the '$' symbol in front of the cell reference.)

For example, consider cell A2 being copied into C7, as shown in Figure 5.

	A	B	C	D	E
1					
2					
3					
4					
5					
6					
7					

Figure 5

- If the contents were =B2 they would become =D7

- If the contents were =$B2 they would become =$B7

- If the contents were =B$2 they would become =D$2

- If the contents were =$B$2 they would become =$B$2.

This is **'absolute addressing'** – if you copy or insert cells, the spreadsheet package does not change the cell references for you. The '$' symbol 'freezes' the part of the reference that follows it.

Worksheets and workbooks

In Excel a spreadsheet is referred to as a **worksheet** and an Excel file is referred to as a **workbook** (a collection of worksheets). When you create a new workbook three blank worksheets are created (Sheet1, Sheet2 and Sheet3). The structure of a workbook is shown in Figure 6.

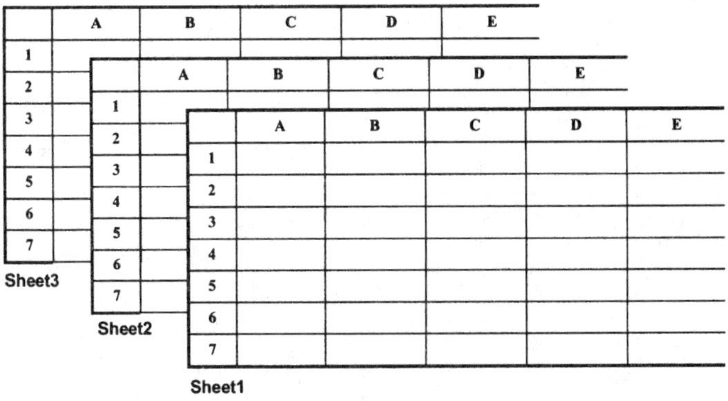

Figure 6

You can insert, move, copy, rename and delete worksheets.

The multiple worksheets in a workbook enable you to build a group of closely related worksheets. Using the example shown in Figure 3, you could have a worksheet for the results for each quarter and a separate worksheet which summarises all the other sheets (and takes all its values from those other sheets).

 ## PUTTING THE BASICS TOGETHER

The following example of a purchase order (Figure 7) shows how some of the common features of a spreadsheet package can be used for an everyday situation.

One of the best ways to understand the workings of spreadsheet packages is to have a go yourself. Try creating the following example and see first hand.

Although this purchase order could have been produced using a word processor, it is much more flexible and user friendly when produced using a spreadsheet. For example, if you change one of the values, such as the number of washers ordered, all the dependent values will change automatically.

	A	B	C	D	E	F	G
1	Purchase order example						
2							
3	Quantity	Description	Part No.	Unit Price (£)	Cost(£)	VAT (£)	Total (£)
4	25	10mm bolts	B10/ss1	0.80	20.00	3.50	23.50
5	25	10mm nuts	N10/ss1	0.25	6.25	1.09	7.34
6	10	Small plates	PL17b	1.25	12.50	2.19	14.69
7	30	10mm washers	W10/ss1	0.12	3.60	0.63	4.23
8							
9	Totals				42.35	7.41	49.76
10		VAT calculated at:		17.50%			

Figure 7

Cell A1 holds the text 'Purchase order example' and has been formatted in bold to give emphasis to the title line. Although it looks as though the title occupies cells A1 and B1, it is contained only in cell A1 (as text). The spreadsheet package recognises that cell B1 is empty and so allows the text to spill in to the display of B1. If, however, B1 was not empty, the display of the text would be truncated to the width available in the cell.

The cells in row 3 hold the heading descriptions for the columns. Column A has been 'centre justified', columns B and C have been 'left justified', and cells D3, E3, F3 and G3 have been 'right justified'. These justifications have been selected so that the titles align with the contents underneath.

Cells D4 to G9 have been formatted as 'number' with two decimal places being displayed.

The 'cost' cells E4 to E7 each contain a formula that multiplies the value in column A with that in column D – for example, cell E4 contains =A4*D4.

Although VAT (at 17.5%) could have been calculated by multiplying the 'cost' by 0.175, it would have meant that the '0.175' was 'hard coded' into the formula so, should the VAT rate change, it would be necessary to change each and every instance of this formula. This could be both a tedious and an error prone process. Therefore the VAT rate has been shown on a separate row with the rate itself in cell D10. Any change to the VAT rate would require a change to just one cell of the spreadsheet.

The contents of cell F4 is now =E4*$D$10. However, to avoid the possibility of rounding errors, the formula should be =ROUND(D5*C13.2). See 'ROUND' on page 51.

Cell D10 has been referenced as $D$10 so that it may be

copied (or dragged) into cells F5, F6 and F7 without losing the specific reference to D10, which otherwise would become D11, D12 and D13. Also, cell D10 contains 17.5%; Excel recognises this as a percentage and the cell is treated as containing the value 0.175 so that if the cell is multiplied with any other cell the right calculation is made.

The totals in cells G4 to G7 are produced by adding the values in columns E and F together. So cell G4 contains =E4+F4. The totals in row 9 use the SUM function to add the values above them. Cell G9 contains =SUM(G4:G8).

KEYPOINTS

✔ Check that the spreadsheet package offers the best solution for your particular piece of work: database and word processing applications also use tables.

✔ To learn what you can achieve from a good spreadsheet, get to know the fundamental capabilities of formulae and functions.

✔ Try putting together the basics in a sample spreadsheet before you begin designing spreadsheets to use.

2 Designing Spreadsheets

A good spreadsheet is easy to use, is presented clearly and contains the right information at the right level. It is designed to be correct, flexible and easy to follow.

4

things you need to know

1 **GENERAL DESIGN CONSIDERATIONS**

2 **DESIGNING FOR THE USER; DESIGNING FOR CHANGE**

3 **STRUCTURING AND FORMATTING**

4 **BEING ACCURATE AND CONSISTENT**

Spreadsheets are easy to produce, look professional but can look 'right' even when they contain mistakes. Whether you use spreadsheets in your personal life (for example, to manage household finances) or in business, if they contain mistakes they can cause you serious problems. Research suggests that as many as half of all spreadsheets contain errors. **It is important to make sure that the spreadsheets you create are 'fit for purpose'.**

Many spreadsheets are created 'on the fly' – decisions about structure, format and other design elements are made as the spreadsheet is being built. This can result in spreadsheets which are difficult to follow, cumbersome to use and change, show too much or too little detail, and the information they contain may be misleading or even wrong. **Good spreadsheets are accurate, intuitive, easy to use and easy to change**; they result from good design.

Good spreadsheet design is about looking beyond the raw calculations within the spreadsheet and thinking about **the purpose of the spreadsheet, who will be using it and how they will be using it**.

 GENERAL DESIGN CONSIDERATIONS

Before you start to build a spreadsheet ask yourself:

- **Who will use it?**

  Are they experienced users?

  Will it always be the same users?

- **What will they use it for?**

  Is it a one-off or will it be used for some time and updated or changed?

  Will they be viewing it on a screen and printing it?

- **How important is the information in it?**

  Should other people be allowed to change, or even to see, the information?

  Can amounts be rounded?

- **What information will I need to build it?**

  Can I get all the information I need?

  How up-to-date will it be?

  Do I need to check how accurate it is?

- **What calculations and formulae will I need?**

  Do I need to check that they are correct?

- **How should I structure and format the information?**

  How should I present the information so that it's clear and easy to follow?

Even if the spreadsheet is only for your own use, or you consider it to be straightforward, you should still think about these points.

The spreadsheet that I received from the finance department certainly looks comprehensive. In fact it's so comprehensive that it takes me ages to find the information I need from it.

For important or complex spreadsheets consider sketching out your design and, if necessary, reviewing it with the intended user or a colleague. If necessary, create a 'mock-up' of the spreadsheet to verify your design.

 DESIGNING FOR THE USER; DESIGNING FOR CHANGE

Even though your spreadsheet is clear to you, it may not be to the person using it or changing it – it may not even be clear to *you* some time after you created it.

Consider the following contents of a cell:

IF(B38="RE","",IF((ISERROR(MATCH("a*",$A$31:$A$40,0))
=TRUE)," ",IF(MATCH("a*",$A$31:$A$40,0)>0,"AMBER","")))

This is a clever instruction that looks for cells which contain 'a' in a range of cells and prints 'AMBER' providing other cells in the range do not contain 'RED'.

However, will other people understand it; indeed will you understand it in several months time?

When you design the spreadsheet think of the user and, because the spreadsheet may be changed, think of the person who has to change it. Simplicity can be more valuable (and less risky) than complexity. Therefore:

● Only carry out a single calculation in a cell – this improves readability and helps to trace mistakes.

- Use industry standard calculations. (Spreadsheet packages usually include a broad set of functions that you can use.)

- Do not use complicated functions unless you are sure they are correct (and that others will be able to understand them and change them if necessary).

- Give names to ranges and use those names in formulae that refer to the ranges.

- Use familiar terms.

- Lay out the information clearly and use colour and other formatting wisely – see Structuring and Formatting on page 25

- Be consistent in what you do – see Being Accurate and Consistent on page 27.

- Consider splitting large spreadsheets into smaller ones which are easier to view on a screen and which can be printed on a single page. (If necessary use a separate sheet for data input.)

Mistakes in spreadsheets are often introduced when you make changes to them – for example, when you insert a new column. Therefore:

- Design the spreadsheet so that you can add rows and columns (and whole spreadsheets if necessary) without harming other parts of it. For example, side-by-side tables may let you get the whole spreadsheet on a screen but it makes inserting extra rows more difficult, as shown in Figure 8. (In this case consider using separate spreadsheets.)

	A	B	C	D	E
1	Council Tax	£ 750.00			
2	Water Rates	£ 150.00		Salary	£1,250.45
3	Car Insurance	£ 275.00		Less housekeeping	−£479.00
4	House Insurance	£ 127.00		Less direct debits	£0.00
5	Housekeeping	£ 479.00		Less provision for car	−£22.92
6	Holiday Fund	£ 1,000.00		Less provision for holiday	−£83.33
7	Other	£ 237.00		Less other provisions	−£19.75
8					
9	**Total budget**	**£ 3,018.00**		**Free cash to spend**	**£645.45**

Figure 8

- Build as many cross-checks into the spreadsheet as you can so that the sheet checks itself.

- If you are repeating information which may change (for example, VAT rates) put it in a separate cell and refer to that cell – then when it changes you only have to change one cell. (The cell can be in the same sheet, in a different sheet in the same workbook, or in a different workbook.)

- If necessary protect cells so that you cannot accidentally overwrite them – for example, cells that contain formulae.

Also, you should **document your spreadsheet** – see Chapter 5.

 ### STRUCTURING AND FORMATTING

The structure and format can make the difference between an effective and an ineffective spreadsheet. **A logical layout with clear titles, the appropriate use of colour**

and fonts all contribute to the 'usability' of a spreadsheet.

However, the over-use of these features can make spreadsheets look fussy and over-complicated. Also, you can spend a lot of time working on the format for little reward so use these features wisely.

A well laid out spreadsheet looks inviting, a poorly laid out one can look hostile.

To make your spreadsheets more useable, consider the following:

Layout

- Use familiar layouts, eg financial information should be in the form of a balance sheet or other accounting format.

- Use separate areas for data entry and data processing and make it clear which is which.

- Show intermediate values – they can help to verify calculations.

- Give clear and concise titles to columns, rows and ranges.

- For large or detailed spreadsheets consider using a separate summary sheet to show results; also think about using charts or graphs to provide user-friendly summaries.

- If information is sorted in a particular order, make sure it is clear to the user.

Colours and borders

- Use colours and border lines to show groupings, functions or relationships between values.

- Allow good contrast between text and background colours – dark colours on a light background are generally better than light colours on a dark background.

- Do not use bright colours for large areas of your spreadsheet.

- Do not use more than six colours if possible.

- Choose colours and shading (patterns) that are clear even when printed in black and white or photocopied.

Fonts

- Use common fonts such as Helvetica or Arial.

- Do not use more than two fonts if possible.

- Do not over-use capitals, italics or underlining – all these can be difficult to read.

- Avoid using very large or very small font sizes – the actual size of the font displayed on a screen will also depend on the size of the screen.

 BEING ACCURATE AND CONSISTENT

The 'professional' look of spreadsheets can make them appear trustworthy – people may assume that they are correct and so act on the information contained in them.

Therefore it is important that your spreadsheet is designed so that:

- the information contained in it is accurate

- the way that you manipulate and present the information is consistent throughout.

Accuracy and consistency make a spreadsheet trustworthy and predictable. People like things that they can trust and anticipate – they can rely on them.

Formatting numbers often causes confusion in spreadsheets. For example the amounts in this spreadsheet are given to two decimal places:

	A	B
1		Sales (£m)
2	Northern region	1.30
3	Southern region	1.40
4	**Total sales**	**2.70**

Figure 9

Formatting the cells B2 to B4 (by choosing Format, Cells from the Menu toolbar) to show the sales figures to the nearest £million (that is, by formatting the cells as numbers with no decimal places) results in:

	A	B
1		Sales (£m)
2	Northern region	1
3	Southern region	1
4	**Total sales**	**3**

Figure 10

Questions may well be asked about the accuracy of your spreadsheet! (This problem can be overcome by using the ROUND function – see page 51.)

Providing accurate information means more than making sure that all the data in it is arithmetically correct. For the information to be accurate you may need to **consider the timing** of it. That is, you may need to make sure that it is sufficiently current for the purpose. (You may need to label your spreadsheet with the dates for which the information is valid.)

You should also consider the clarity of the information. For example, if a spreadsheet contains a 'Total cost' field, is it clear if the cost includes VAT? And if so, what is the rate of VAT (especially if the VAT rate has just changed or is about to change)?

If your spreadsheet contains information that you have received from another source you may need to check its accuracy with whoever gave it to you.

Modern spreadsheet packages offer a wide range of complex and sophisticated functions and features, and the same results can often be achieved in many different ways. **Spreadsheets are easier to follow if they are consistent**. Consistency should cover all aspects of your spreadsheet including:

- the way that you calculate values

- the layout and format

- the use of labels

- headings and other text

- help messages

- consistency with other, similar spreadsheets

- consistency with industry, company and other standards.

If you are changing a spreadsheet that someone else has created, use the standards, styles and checks that they have used unless there is a good reason not to.

KEYPOINTS

✔ Before starting to create your spreadsheet make sure you know who its users will be and its purpose.

✔ Design your spreadsheet so that it is clear to the user and can be changed simply .

✔ Structure and format your spreadsheet in a way that makes it easy to follow.

✔ Make sure the information is accurate and that it is presented consistently.

3 Building Spreadsheets Step-by-Step

Taking a business-like approach to building spreadsheets reduces the risk of errors. Cutting corners can result in ambiguity or even mistakes. The more important the spreadsheet, the more important it is well built.

5 things you need to know

1 **ENTERING HEADINGS**

2 **FORMATTING CELLS**

3 **USING FORMULAE AND FUNCTIONS**

4 **ENTERING DATA**

5 **CHECKING YOUR SPREADSHEET**

A well-built spreadsheet fulfils all the design criteria for that spreadsheet. The purpose of each cell is clear (for example, by the use of appropriate headings), cells are formatted according to the data that they will contain, formulae and functions are used correctly and any of the useful features of spreadsheets (such as charts) are used wisely. Above all, the spreadsheet is checked to make sure that it is **free from errors** and **works in the way that the user would expect**.

Most spreadsheets need to be changed at some point; rows or columns may need to be inserted, formulae may need revising or additional features may need to be incorporated. Spreadsheets that are well designed and carefully built can be easier to change in the future.

What might start as a one-off spreadsheet often becomes a long-lasting, significant office component. As the previous chapter indicated, even if the spreadsheet is only for your own use, or you consider it straightforward, still spend some time thinking about the design before building it.

Whether you are building a spreadsheet from scratch or amending an existing spreadsheet, follow some basic steps to make sure that those spreadsheets are 'fit for purpose'.

① ENTERING HEADINGS

Headings (or titles) in a spreadsheet are like direction signs to a driver; they give important guidance.

Each column that contains data should have a **heading**, unless it is obvious to the user what the column contains. For example, a heading of 'Cost' gives no indication of whether the cost includes VAT so a more explicit heading of 'Cost (excl. VAT)' is more helpful. However, the placement of a column can imply the contents of the column itself. For example, a column headed 'Cost' followed immediately by a column headed 'VAT' implies that the 'Cost' column excludes VAT. Nevertheless, **if you want to avoid ambiguity, be explicit**.

Also, for large spreadsheets, you can 'freeze' rows and columns on the screen so that they always appear in the same place when you scroll down or across the spreadsheet. (*How*: To freeze rows, select the row below the rows that you want to freeze and then from the Menu toolbar choose Window, Freeze Panes. You can freeze columns in a similar way. To freeze rows and columns at the same time, select the cell to the right of the column and below the row. To unfreeze, from the Menu toolbar choose Window, Unfreeze Panes).

For example, to freeze the first three rows and first two columns in the spreadsheet shown in Figure 11, select cell C4 and follow the instruction given above.

	A	B	C	D	E	F	G
1	Purchase order example						
2							
3	Quantity	Description	Part No.	Unit price (£)	Cost(£)	VAT (£)	Total (£)
4	25	10mm bolts	B10/ss1	0.80	20.00	3.50	23.50
5	25	10mm nuts	N10/ss1	0.25	6.25	1.09	7.34
6	10	Small plates	PL17b	1.25	12.50	2.19	14.69
7	30	10mm washers	W10/ss1	0.12	3.60	0.63	4.23
8							
9	Totals				42.35	7.41	49.76
10		VAT calculated at:		17.50%			

Figure 11

Sub-totals, totals and other summary information should also be labelled clearly.

It may be appropriate to indicate the way in which values have been produced. For example, in a column headed 'Delivery charge' you could use a note to show how the charge is calculated. You can add a note to a cell so that when the cursor is over the cell the note is displayed. (*How*: Select the cell for which you want the note. Then from the Menu toolbar, choose Insert, Note.)

By default, text is left justified and numbers are right justified. Therefore, you may need to align column headings and column contents. See Formatting Cells on page 35.

In addition to giving headings to rows and columns, you should also give a heading to each spreadsheet. Furthermore, if your spreadsheet will be printed, each page should also include a heading. You should also consider including additional information such as:

● the date that the spreadsheet was last updated (that is, an 'as at' date) or last printed

● the time that the spreadsheet was last updated or printed

● the version of the spreadsheet

● the name and location of the file

● the page number (and if appropriate the total number of pages - for example, 1 of 6)

● the name of the person who created/updated the spreadsheet.

There are two ways that you can include headings and related information on spreadsheets that you print (and you can use both ways at the same time).

(i) You can specify rows to be repeated at the top of the page and columns to be repeated on the left hand side of the page; you can include your headings in those rows and columns. With this option the headings will appear on the screen and on the printed version.

(ii) You can specify headers and footers which appear at the top and bottom of all pages respectively. You can also include information (such as filename, page numbers, date and time) and the information is automatically updated each time the spreadsheet is printed. However, with this option the headings will appear only on the printed version.

A combination of both options is, in many cases, the most appropriate.

② FORMATTING CELLS

The ability to format cells gives you control over how the contents of cells are displayed on a screen and printed.

The apparent contents of a cell (as it appears on the screen or printed) can be different from the actual content of the cell, and it is the formatting of the cell which is responsible for this difference. For example, a cell appears to contain the numeric 13, however on closer inspection it actually contains 12.75; the cell is formatted as a numeric cell with no decimal places – that is, it is rounded to the nearest whole number. (The actual contents of the cell are shown in the formula bar when the cell is selected.)

Effective spreadsheets can be developed without the need for elaborate formatting.

The format that you apply to a cell will depend on its purpose and the default settings may be appropriate for many situations. In general, you should apply the following guidelines:

- Numbers should be right justified (– it's the default)

- Text should be left justified (– it's the default). However, text which is a heading should be justified so that it is consistent with the cells associated with it.

There are comprehensive formatting options for cells, including:

- number – which itself provides a selection of options, including:
  - currency
  - accounting (which align decimal points)
  - date

- time
- percentage
- fraction
- scientific
- text
- special (such as phone number)
- custom

● alignment (horizontal and vertical) and orientation (for example, text upright or on its side)

● font (style, size and colour)

● border (around the cell, including thickness and colour)

● pattern (cell colour and shading)

● protection (to hide cells and lock cells – for example, to prevent changes being made to cells that contain formulae).

Also, you can format rows and columns (including height and width respectively) as well as defining the background for worksheets.

You can carry out the same action (such as formatting) on ranges of cells that are not next to each other. (*How*: Select one range and then hold down Ctrl while you select the other ranges.)

Many spreadsheet packages have an 'Autoformat' feature which offers a choice of styles that you can apply to your spreadsheet. You can also define your own styles and apply them to other spreadsheets. They also have a selection of spreadsheet templates which you can use when you create a spreadsheet.

Be aware that the spreadsheet may be printed so any features that are screen-specific (such as freezing panes) will not apply when the spreadsheet is printed and they may make the printed spreadsheet difficult or confusing to read.

 USING FORMULAE AND FUNCTIONS

The precedence within formulae

In formulae which contain more than one operator, the operators are evaluated according to an order of precedence.

For example, if a cell contains:

=1+2*3

the result will be 7. (The operation of multiplication takes precedence over the operation of addition.) However, if the cell contains:

= (1+2)*3

the result will be 9.

If you are not sure about the order in which operations will be carried out, use brackets (parentheses) to impose the order.

Here is the order in which the main mathematical operations are carried out.

Mathematical operations

Precedence	Operation	Symbol
1st	Parentheses	( )
2nd	Negation (eg –1)	–
3rd	Percentages	%
4th	Exponentiation (ie raising to a power)	^
5th	Multiplication and division	*, /
6th	Addition and subtraction	+, –

If a formula contains two operations of the same level (such as multiplication and division) then the operations are calculated in the order in which they occur (that is, from left to right). **Use brackets if you want to override the order.**

Using built-in functions

Before building your own functions, first check to see if your spreadsheet package already has the function built in. If it does, use it in preference to building your own.

Here are some of the built-in functions.

- **Mathematical functions**: trigonometric functions (such as Sine, Cosine and Tangent), logarithmic and exponential functions, rounding functions and a random number generator.

- **Statistical functions**: average, minimum, maximum, median and modal values in a list, distributions (such as Normal and Gamma) and related functions (such as Standard deviation).

- **Financial functions**: accrued interest, asset depreciation, future values of investments, cash flow analyses (Net Present Value and Internal Rate of Return) and coupon calculations (such as number of days to settlement date).

- **Logical functions**: If, And, Or, Not, True and False.

- **Engineering functions**: complex numbers, the Bessel function and conversion between measurement systems (such as from binary to hexadecimal).

- **Text functions**: converting text to lower or upper case, finding or replacing one text value within another, removing spaces from text, repeating text and joining separate pieces of text together.

- **Information functions**: details of the contents of cells (such as whether a cell contains an even number).

- **Date and time functions**: current date and time, number of days between two given dates and the conversion of serial numbers to days of the month.

(There are also add-ins available which include more specialist functions.)

Some popular functions are discussed in more detail on page 48.

You can insert formulae into a cell and automatically reproduce the formula in many other cells at the same time – taking advantage of relative addressing – refer back to page 15 for more about relative addressing. (*How*: Select the cell that contains the formula you want to reproduce and then hold down Ctrl while you drag the 'fill handle' which is at the bottom right hand corner of the cell; the cell must have a formula in it.)

Before you reproduce formulae, check that they work.

And remember, if you insert rows or columns which should be included in any existing formulae, you should check that the formulae do actually cover the new cells.

 ENTERING DATA

Entering **data** usually involves selecting the cell into which the data is to go and typing it in. However, this can often be a slow and tedious process and in many cases there are alternative, more efficient approaches available, especially if the source data is already in electronic form. For example, you can:

- **Copy and paste** from other packages. For example, by using the Clipboard in Windows (Ctrl C to copy and Ctrl V to paste).

- **Import data** from other packages. For example, there are facilities to import data from database files (such as Access, dBase and Paradox).

Even if you have formatted cells, you may still be able to key in data in another format. For example, if you enter 24-08-00 into a cell which is formatted as a date in the form DD-MMM-YYYY the contents of the cell is displayed as 24-Aug-2000.

You may also be able to apply some **data validation rules** so that only data which conforms to those rules is accepted. Using the above date example, you could specify that dates must be within the range 01-07-00 – 31-12-00.

Using automated techniques to enter data can help to reduce the amount of keying and the risk of keying errors.

So, for example, if you are creating a holiday chart and you already have a list of staff in a Word document, you can copy and paste the list without having to re-key the names.

Some spreadsheet packages provide an **'autofill'** facility in which you enter the first few entries of a series and the package automatically fills in the rest of the series. You can automatically create a series of numbers, dates, times and other values using the 'AutoFill' facility. For example, 1,2,3 . . . 10 or Jan, Feb . . . Dec. (*How*: Select the cell that you want to start from and then hold down Ctrl while you drag the 'fill handle' which is at the bottom right hand corner of the cell; the cell must have a number in it.)

Also, you can automatically correct words that are not spelt correctly, or expand abbreviated words. (*How*: From the Menu toolbar, choose Tools, Autocorrect.)

You should enter data into your spreadsheet after you have entered all the formulae, headings and other information which should not change. If necessary, you can then protect the cells which you do not want changed (such as cells which contain formulae), especially if other people will be using your spreadsheet. You may also want to consider separating cells which users should be able to change (such as data input cells) from cells which they should not be able to change (such as cells containing formulae).

In practice the building of a spreadsheet can sometimes be an iterative process which involves changes after the spreadsheet is populated with data. Often change involves having to insert rows or columns into a spreadsheet; make sure that any rows and columns you insert are reflected in

	A	B
1	**Region**	**Sales (£K)**
2	North	13
3	South	15
4	East	19
5	West	12
6	**Total**	**59**

Figure 12

any related formulae. Consider the example in Figure 12. Cell B6 contains the formula:

=SUM(B2:B5).

Figure 13 shows the result of inserting a new row after row 5.

	A	B
1	**Region**	**Sales (£K)**
2	North	13
3	South	15
4	East	19
5	West	12
6	Central	11
7	**Total**	**59**

Figure 13

Cell B7 contains the formula:

=SUM(B2:B5).

The total in cell B7 must be updated manually to contain:

=SUM(B2:B6).

Similarly, inserting the row after row 1 would also exclude it from the total which would become B7 and which would contain:

=SUM(B3:B6).

However, inserting the new row between row 1 and row 5 in Figure 12 would mean that it is included automatically in the total, which would contain:

=SUM(B2:B6).

If you make changes to a spreadsheet, make sure they are incorporated in any formulae, headings and so on.

⑤ CHECKING YOUR SPREADSHEET

Checking your spreadsheet means making sure that it is **fit for purpose**. You should check that it is:

● accurate

● consistent

● well structured

● clear.

The more important a spreadsheet is, the more thoroughly you should check it.

The amount of checking that you do will depend on a number of factors, including:

- How important the spreadsheet is.

- Who will use it. If other people will be using it, consider their knowledge of spreadsheet packages.

- How it will be used. For example, will it be printed as well as viewed on screen?

Here are some of the techniques that you can use to check your spreadsheet:

Use cross-checks

Consider the example in Figure 14.

	A	B	C	D	E	F
1			Sales (£K)			
2	**Region**	**Q1**	**Q2**	**Q3**	**Q4**	**Year total**
3	North	13	11	9	11	44
4	South	15	14	15	17	61
5	East	19	23	22	25	89
6	West	12	10	10	11	43
7	Central	11	11	9	10	41
8	**Totals**	**70**	**69**	**65**	**74**	**278**

Figure 14

The contents of cell F8 can be either:

=SUM(F3:F7)

or

=SUM(B8:E8).

Differences could occur if the cells being summed have been rounded.

Whichever of the two options you choose you could (in a cell outside the range) check that both sums are the same. For example, if you choose =SUM(F3:F7), you could include in cell G8 the following formula:

=IF(G8=SUM(B8:E8),,'Check year totals against quarter totals').

(The IF function is discussed on page 51).

You may have spotted that there is a third way to calculate the contents of cell F8, namely =SUM(B3:E7). However, using this calculation could, again because of rounding, produce a result which differs from the sum of the quarter totals or the sum of the region totals.

Input test values

For example:

- put a value of '1' in every input cell and look for problems in totals and cross-checks

- put minimum and maximum values into every input cell and check the results

- put values in which check both the 'true' and 'false' results of IF functions.

If there are links to or from other spreadsheets, make sure that those links work in the way that you expect. For example, if your spreadsheet picks up a value from another spreadsheet, check that changes to those values are included in your spreadsheet.

Also, if you make changes to your spreadsheet and another spreadsheet picks up values from it, check that the other spreadsheet includes the changes – or ask the owner of the other spreadsheet to check it.

Don't restrict yourself to the values that you would expect to be input to the spreadsheet; think also of the unexpected values. (For example, if you format a range of cells to be dates with a format DD-MMM-YY, what happens if someone enters 30-02-01 – 30th February 2001?)

Ask other people to check it

Ask a colleague to check it. If other people will be using it, ask them to check it too – it can also be a useful way for them to get to know it.

You can audit your spreadsheet using tools provided with the package. For example, you can use 'tracers' to quickly and easily discover the source of any mistakes. (*How*: From the Menu toolbar, choose Tools, Auditing, Show Auditing Toolbar.)

KEYPOINTS

✔ Give explicit, unambiguous headings to columns and rows, and to the spreadsheet itself.

✔ Be consistent with the way that you format cells.

✔ Get to know the precedence of operations within formulae.

✔ Use your spreadsheet package's built-in functions rather than building your own.

✔ Discover and use the most efficient ways of entering data.

✔ Use cross-checks, input test values and ask other people to check your spreadsheet.

4 Practical Spreadsheet Features

Using built-in features of spreadsheet packages, such as charts, drawings and other features, can bring your spreadsheets to life.

Spreadsheet packages come jammed with features designed to make life easier. For example, the **built-in functions** can reduce the risk of error and improve efficiency – you don't waste time deriving the functions. Some packages even give you step-by-step guidance.

However, the power of spreadsheets does not stop at formulae and functions. Packages are now expected to provide **comprehensive graphical features** (such as the ability to produce charts and graphs from spreadsheets), **macros** (sets of instructions that are likely to be carried out many times) and even **database facilities** (eg, providing the ability to find, add, amend and delete data using on-line forms). Furthermore, the ability to produce spreadsheet data in a form suitable for publishing on a web site is becoming a necessary, rather than just a desirable, feature.

These features can be extremely powerful. They can

bring authority and professionalism to your business communications. However, they can also be overused and result in spreadsheets which are over-engineered, unnecessarily complex and difficult to maintain. **Great spreadsheets use these features wisely**.

 POPULAR BUILT-IN FUNCTIONS

The following are popular built-in spreadsheet functions:

- SUM

- COUNT

- IF

- ROUND

- NOW

Sum

SUM is probably the most widely used function. Its basic structure (or syntax) is:

=SUM(value 1, value 2, . . ., value n)

and you can have up to 30 values. Values can be numbers, cell references and ranges.

As well as summing simple ranges such as =SUM(A1:A7), disjointed ranges can also be summed. For example, you can sum the shaded ranges in Figure 15 by using the formula: =SUM(A1:A7,C1:C7,E1:E7).

There is also an Autosum feature which can automatically calculate the sum of a range of cells. (*How*: Select the range and click on the Autosum button, Σ, on the standard toolbar. The result is placed in the cell next to the range.)

The SUMIF function, as the name suggests, combines the SUM and IF functions (the IF function is discussed on page

	A	B	C	D	E
1					
2					
3					
4					
5					
6					
7					

Figure 15

51). It addresses a common business situation summing a list of values which meet specific criteria.

In the example in Figure 16, rows 16 and 17 show the result of offering a 5% discount on an order line of 50 or more items. Cell D16 contains:
=SUMIF(A4:A10,">=50",E4:E10).
This will sum the value in the range E4 to E10 if the corresponding value in the range A4 to A10 is greater than or equal to 50; in this example 52.00 and 46.00.

Or line items over £50 may qualify for discount in which case the result would be as shown in Figure 17.

Cell D16 contains =SUMIF(E4:E10,">=50",E4:E10).

This is very similar to the above example but the same range is specified for both searching and summing. In this example it finds the values 52.00 and 62.50.

	A	B	C	D	E	F	G
1	**Purchase order example**						
2		All amounts in £					
3	Quantity	Description	Part no.	Unit price	Cost	VAT	Total
4	100	8mm nuts	N8/ssa4	0.52	52.00	9.10	61.10
5	20	12mm nuts	N12/ssa2	0.74	14.80	2.59	17.39
6	50	12mm nuts	N12/ssa4	0.92	46.00	8.05	54.05
7	25	10mm bolts	B10/ss1	0.80	20.00	3.50	23.50
8	25	10mm nuts	N10/ss1	0.25	6.25	1.09	7.34
9	10	Small plates	PL17b	6.25	62.50	10.94	73.44
10	30	10mm washers	W10/ss1	0.12	3.60	0.63	4.23
11							
12	Totals				205.15	35.90	241.05
13							
14		VAT rate:	17.5%				
15							
16		Amount qualifying for discount		98.00			
17		Discount at:	5%	4.90			

Figure 16

	A	B	C	D	E	F	G
16		Amount qualifying for discount		114.50			
17		Discount at:	5%	5.73			

Figure 17

Count

As the name suggests the COUNT function counts values in a range – more specifically, the number of numeric values in a range.

The basic structure of the function is:

=COUNT(value 1, value 2, . . ., value n)

and you can have up to 30 values. Values can be numbers, cell references and ranges.

Using the example in Figure 16:

=COUNT(A4:A10) would produce the result 7.

There are several variations of the function and these cover the most popular needs of most spreadsheet users. The variations are:

- COUNTA counts text values in the range

- COUNTBLANK counts blank cells in the range

- COUNTIF counts values in the range which meet the criteria specified. For example,
  =COUNTIF(A4:A10,">=100") would produce the result 1.

If

The IF function provides the ability to determine the contents of a cell based on the contents of other cells. The structure of the function is:

=IF(logical test, value if true, value if false).

For example, in Figure 17, if discounts were tiered so that for orders up to £500 the discount is 5% and for orders of more than £500 the discount is 10%, the contents of cell C17 would be:

=IF(D16 < = 500,5%,10%).

The IF function offers a very simple but powerful capability which has many practical applications.

Round

The basic structure of the function is:

=ROUND(value, number of digits)

and it rounds the 'value' specified according to the 'number of digits' specified. So,

= Round (19.66,1)

gives the result 19.7.

The way that the value is rounded depends on the 'number of digits' specified.

'Number of digits' specified	Action taken on the value
Greater than zero	rounds to the number of decimal points given by the 'number of digits'. For example =ROUND(37.238,2) results in 37.24
Equal to zero	rounds to the nearest integer For example =ROUND(37.238,0) results in 37
Less than zero	rounds to the left of the decimal point For example =ROUND(37.238,-1) results in 40

What is the value of the ROUND function? Consider the example in Figure 18.

The formula in column E is in the form =ROUND(D5*$C$13,2) which gives the 'correct' results (in relation to the formula in column G which is in the simpler form =D5*$C$13).

The printed results of the VAT calculations in columns E and G are the same, but, the SUMs in E12 and G12 differ by one penny. The reason is made clearer by the values in column H, which are calculated in the same way as those in column G, although they are formatted to three decimal places instead of the usual two.

The problem with column G is that the 'Format Cells' feature rounds up the printed versions of the calculations

	A	B	C	D	E	F	G	H
1	Purchase order example							
2								
3	Quantity	Description	Unit price (£)	Cost (£)	VAT (£)	Total (£)	VATx	VATy
4								
5	20	10mm nuts	0.25	5.00	0.88	5.88	0.88	0.875
6	20	8mm nuts	0.24	4.80	0.84	5.64	0.84	0.840
7	20	6mm nuts	0.23	4.60	0.81	5.41	0.81	0.805
8	20	5mm nuts	0.22	4.40	0.77	5.17	0.77	0.770
9	10	Small plates	1.25	12.50	2.19	14.69	2.19	2.188
10	30	10mm washers	0.12	3.60	0.63	4.23	0.63	0.630
11								
12	Totals			34.90	6.12	41.02	6.11	6.11
13		VAT rate:	17.50%					

Figure 18

but the internal values still (correctly) retain their true precision.

The ROUND function operates on the internal values of the cells and 'rounds' them so that they are consistent with their printed values.

A one-penny discrepancy in this example may not seem something to get excited about. However, as you encounter more complex examples the role of ROUND function becomes more important. For example, if you use the IF function to compare two values and then take some specified action, make sure cells that print the same, are the same, unless you wish to spend many frustrating hours wondering why your formulae won't give the expected results!

When you compare the contents of cells E5 and G5, both

of which print as 0.88, they will not compare equal. This is because cell G5 really contains 0.875. Most spreadsheet packages have an option on the basic ROUND function to permit rounding-up, rounding-down and other variants.

Now

NOW is one of the many time-related functions. The syntax of the function is:

=NOW().

There are no input parameters (that is, arguments). The result is the current date and time in the format

DD/MM/YYYY HH:MM

for example, 27/10/2000 12:19.

You can change the format by formatting the cell as a date – which provides a range of popular date formats.

 USEFUL FEATURES

Most spreadsheet packages have a large selection of useful features. This section gives a flavour of some of the many which can enhance the efficiency, usability and overall effectiveness of your spreadsheets.

Sorting

There are likely to be many occasions when you will want to sort the information in a spreadsheet. If, for example, you have used the database facility (see page 61) to input data into a spreadsheet, the data will be put at the end of the existing data. So if your spreadsheet contains a list of people's names you may want to sort the list by last names. (*How*: To sort a range, select the range and from the Menu toolbar choose Data, Sort.)

There are usually a number of options available on which

to sort, including:

- the data on which the sort should be based (such as last name, then first name)

- the order in which the data should be sorted – ascending or descending

- whether or not the case of text is relevant (for sorting upper case and lower case text)

- whether the data should be sorted top to bottom (for columns) or left to right (for rows).

And you can identify headings in the data which should be excluded from the sort.

You can also specify certain types of data, such as dates, that you would not want sorted according to conventional rules. For example, if you wanted to sort months of the year, you would not do it alphabetically – you can specify the data as being months of the year. (*How*: From the Menu toolbar choose Data, Sort, Options, and choose the type of data from the 'First key sort order' drop-down box.)

Hiding rows and columns

The ability to hide rows or columns means that you can mask intermediate calculations and other information which may be useful to you but not to those who are using your spreadsheet.

How: To hide a column – select the column, or a cell within a column. From the Menu toolbar choose Format, Column, Hide. A quicker way is to reduce the width of the column so that it is no longer in view – place the cursor in the column heading and drag the right-hand side of the column to the left.

To unhide columns select the column either side of the hidden column. From the Menu toolbar choose Format, Column, Unhide. You can hide rows in the same way.

Hiding rows and columns is particularly useful on printed spreadsheets where paper size puts a restriction on space. However, some people argue that by hiding rows or columns you may increase people's curiosity about what you are concealing. People can spend time finding out how to redisplay the hidden rows/columns.

Using goal seek

'If we need to increase our profits by 10%, what effect could it have on our minimum charge figure?'

Goal seek provides a 'what if' capability which enables you to keep putting different values into your spreadsheets and watching the recalculation until you get the answer you are looking for.

Consider the example in Figure 19. The company's overall sales figures are lower than the target which they set themselves of a 5% increase.

They could use goal seek to determine, for example, what the North region's current sales figures (cell C3) would have to be to meet the overall 5% target. (*How*: From the Menu toolbar choose Tools, Goal seek.)

Goal seek only allows you to consider the effect on a single variable which may be inappropriate for many business situations. Excel includes an add-in (that is, a function in addition to the standard set) called Solver which enables you to view possible impacts on more than one cell. For example, in Figure 19 you might want to consider how the North region's and East region's current sales figures

	A	B	C	D
1		Sales (£K)		
2	Region	Previous year	Current year	% change
3	North	13	12	-7.7
4	South	15	17	13.3
5	East	19	19	0
6	West	12	13	8.3
7	Total	59	61	3.4

Figure 19

(cells C3 and C5 respectively) would between them contribute to meeting the overall 5% target. (*How*: From the Menu toolbar choose Tools, Goal seek and follow the instructions.)

 USING CHARTS AND GRAPHS

Spreadsheets can carry important information but it is often buried in a sea of numbers. Some people are adept at reviewing information in spreadsheet format but others are put off. The ability to summarise information in graphic form can have great appeal, especially if that information is to be included in presentation material (such as business cases, reports and sales literature). **It is easier to absorb information which is presented graphically**.

One of the great strengths of the charting facility is that if you make a change to the underlying data in the worksheet, the chart is updated automatically.

There is a broad range of built-in formats of charts and graphs including:

- bar charts

- line charts

- pie charts

- scatter charts

- radar charts

- surface charts

- bubble charts

as well as the ability to customise the standard built-in charts.

Also some charts can be displayed in two-dimensional or three-dimensional form.

Figure 20 shows the result of creating a two-dimensional line chart of the sales information given in Figure 19. The

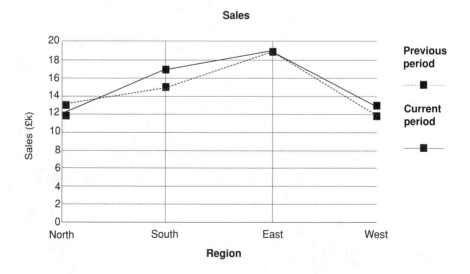

Figure 20

range selected to create the chart was A2:C6; the row and
column labels are picked up automatically as they are
included in the range.

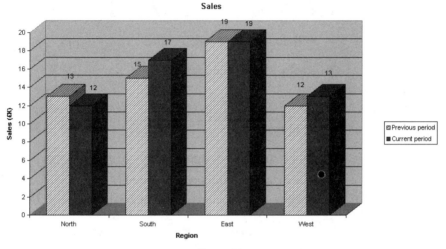

Figure 21

Figure 21 shows the result of creating a three-
dimensional column chart again using the sales information
given in Figure 19.

As well as being able to change the format of graphs, you
can control the colours, labels and other aspects.

 ADVANCED FEATURES

Most spreadsheet packages provide **features which extend
further the power of spreadsheets**. Although some of
these can appear relatively complex, others can be
mastered quite quickly.

Two popular features are **macros** and **databases.**

Macros

A macro is a set of instructions that you are likely to carry
out many times. It is a time-saving device and, because you

only need to create a macro once, you avoid the risks of making mistakes whilst repeatedly carrying out the same set of tasks. You could, for example, create a macro to:

- sort the rows of a spreadsheet

- format a range of cells

- create a header and footer

- print a spreadsheet

- all of the above.

Also, you can define a shortcut key (for example, Ctrl+K) to run the macro and thereby save you even more time.

There are two ways that you can create a macro:

- Record the macro. This is similar to recording something with a tape recorder – you tell the package to start recording, it records your keystrokes and mouse clicks, and then you tell it to stop recording. (*How*: From the Menu toolbar choose Tools, Record New Macro. Give the macro a name, click OK – select Options to define a shortcut key – and anything you do after that will be recorded until you stop recording. To stop recording – From the Menu toolbar choose Tools, Record Macro, Stop Recording.)

- Write the macro. Macro instructions are the instructions of a programming language, VBA (Visual Basic for Applications). The built-in functions are also a set of VBA instructions – they perform a task and give you the result.

Written macros offer much greater flexibility over recorded macros. For example, the actions of a recorded macro cannot be determined by the contents of a cell (such as, 'if cell A >0 then do Y, else do Z) whereas they can be with a written macro.

Programming using VBA requires an additional set of concepts and associated terminology beyond the scope of this book.

Databases

In Excel a database is a list of related rows and columns on which you can carry out actions. For example, you can:

- sort the list (and base the sort on more than one of the items in the list)

- find, add, change or delete items in the list

- define 'forms' which act as an interface to the list; you can use these forms to find, add, change or delete items in the list

- define 'views' of the list (such as specific subsets of the data in the list).

For example, you could set up a list of your business contacts, as in Figure 22 on the next page.

You can automatically generate a form which you can then use to maintain the list. (*How*: Click on any cell in the list, from the Menu toolbar choose Data, Form.) Figure 23 shows a form which is used to maintain the list from Figure 22 – it shows the first entry in the database list – that is, row 4.

You can use the Criteria facility to search for records which meet the criteria which you specify. (*How*: Click on the Criteria button, and key the search criteria into the

	A	B	C	D	E	F	G	H	I
1			**Business contacts**						
2									
3	**Last name**	**First name**	**Company name**	**Street**	**Town**	**Postcode**	**Telephone**	**e-mail**	**web site**
4	Hill	David	Basic Bolts Ltd	Station Road	Hertford	SG08 4QQ	02344-973009	dh@basicbol tsltd.com	www.useful co.com
5	Kate	Elizabeth	Block Technologies	2, The Hill	Plymouth	PL12 2BB	01752-444555	kate@btech_ plymouth.co.uk	www.btech_ plymouth.co.uk
6	Law	Lindsay	R Supplies	The Mill	Stirling	FK9 7UU	01786-234334	law@rsupps. co.uk	www.supps. co.uk

Figure 22

appropriate fields in the blank form. For example, you can search for all contacts in Hertford by keying Hertford in the Town field.) The labels (First name, Company name, etc. in Figure 23) are automatically picked up as being column headings in the list.

You can use the full range of comparison operators (=, <, >, <=, >= and <>) when you use the Criteria facility.

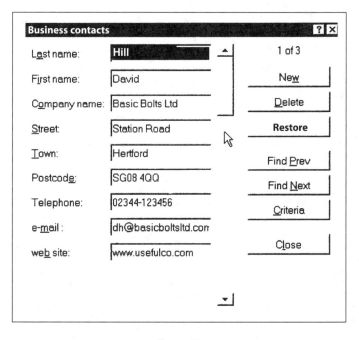

Figure 23

KEYPOINTS

✔ Improve your efficiency by using the most apropriate built-in functions.

✔ Features like sorting, hiding rows and columns, and goal seek enhance usability.

✔ Summarise spreadsheet information graphically to make it easily understood.

✔ Knowing about advanced features can save time and cut down on errors.

5 Managing Spreadsheets

*Important spreadsheets should be managed in a
similar way to other important business applications.
Good spreadsheets deserve good management.*

3

things you need
to know

1 **MANAGING INFORMATION**

2 **CONTROLLING ACCESS AND CHANGES**

3 **DOCUMENTING YOUR SPREADSHEET**

Many spreadsheets are created for a single purpose or event. However, over time they grow to become important business systems which can form a fundamental part of a business process. Spreadsheets are produced using 'end-user' packages and tend not to attract the same level of management and control as other more prominent business systems, such as central accounting systems. Nevertheless, spreadsheets are exposed to many of the same risks as other important systems and **you should manage your spreadsheets in line with their level of importance**.

Managing your spreadsheets means more than just making a back-up copy of them. For example, you also need to make sure that they are up-to-date, accessible to the people who need to use them and protected from unauthorised access or use. Also, control any changes that are applied to them. Important spreadsheets should also be documented appropriately.

A number of factors can determine the level to which you manage a spreadsheet, including how often it is used, the value of the data it contains and the use it is put to.

 MANAGING INFORMATION

If your spreadsheet contains important information and you lose it or it is not correct, it could put you and your business in a very difficult position. Therefore **take steps to make sure that the information contained in your spreadsheet is managed appropriately.**

- Make sure someone has overall responsibility for the spreadsheet. This is particularly important if it is shared.

- Have at least one back-up copy of your spreadsheet which is kept separate from the master. Make sure that you can access your back-up copies if you need to.

- Keep master and back-up copies secure (from unauthorised access, fire and other risks).

- Replace the back-up copy if you update the master. Don't overwrite the previous back-up copy in case you need to refer to it (for example, if you discover a problem with the current version).

- Keep up-to-date documentation about your spreadsheet – see Documenting Your Spreadsheet on page 70.

- If your spreadsheet contains any confidential information protect it by controlling access. Confidential information is information which could be harmful or embarrassing to you or others if disclosed. (See Controlling Access page 68.)

The more important a spreadsheet is, the more important it is to manage the information within it.

Modern spreadsheet packages allow you to share information between spreadsheets. For example, in a formula you can refer to cells in another file (workbook); the spreadsheet automatically picks up the cell contents without you even having to open the other file. This means that you can have access to the most up-to-date information as well as avoiding duplication of information (and the associated management of more than one copy of that information).

As well as sharing information between spreadsheets, you can link to spreadsheets from other applications. For example, if you create a business case in a word processed document you can embed (within the document) your cash flow analysis as a spreadsheet. Any changes you make to the spreadsheet are automatically included in the version embedded (contained) in the Word document.

The ability to link spreadsheets and to embed them in other applications is a powerful facility. However, it means that you may be using information from a spreadsheet that you do not control; any changes to the spreadsheet that you are linking to will also be included in your results, and so could have an adverse effect on those results. **If the source, or the timeliness, of information is important you should consider including the source, version number, date and, if necessary, the time that the spreadsheet was last updated.**

Many countries have laws about the information that you can store electronically and how you can use that information. For example, in England and Wales, if your spreadsheets contain personal data make sure that you keep to the Data Protection principles. These state that personal data must be:

- obtained, used and processed fairly and lawfully

- held only for specifically registered purposes

- used and disclosed consistently with those purposes

- adequate, relevant and not excessive

- kept accurate and up-to-date

- not kept longer than necessary

- made available to the individual concerned and be corrected or erased if justified

- kept secure against unauthorised access, loss, disclosure or destruction.

Companies have to register all the ways they use personal data. Many spreadsheets are created which contain personal data (such as staff details). If you have a spreadsheet that contains personal data you must make sure that it is registered – many companies have a Data Protection representative.

 ## CONTROLLING ACCESS AND CHANGES

Controlling access

One of the easiest ways to control access to your spreadsheet is to **password-protect** it. You can assign a password to a workbook so that only those people who know the password can open your spreadsheet. (*How*: From the Menu toolbar choose File, Save As, click on the Options button and enter a password in the Protection Password box.)

Warning: If you protect an Excel file with a password and then forget the password, you will not be able to open the file, access the information in it or remove the password protection. Consider keeping a list of passwords; if you do, keep it in a safe place.

You can control access by storing it in an area which is itself controlled, as you can with any other computer file – for example, by storing it on your C: drive and password protecting your PC. If you use a network you can use the permissions associated with the various drives of the network.

If your spreadsheet contains confidential information, protect it before sending it as an attachment to an e-mail message.

Controlling changes

Even though you may want to give people access to your spreadsheet you may also want to prevent changes being made to it, either intentionally or unintentionally. You can allow other people to see, but not change, your spreadsheet. (*How*: From the Menu toolbar choose File, Save As, click on the Options button and enter a password in the Write Reservation Password box.) You can also protect worksheets, ranges and cells.

At some point you may have to make changes to your spreadsheet. **Take steps to make sure those changes are controlled.** Here are some of the steps that you can take.

● Do not overwrite an existing version of your spreadsheet with changes. Create a new version instead. If you subsequently discover that changes were applied incorrectly, you can return to the previous version.

- If necessary make a copy before you update the cell contents (or any formulae, macros or other parts) of the spreadsheet so that you can return to a known position if things go wrong.

- Give version numbers to each spreadsheet.

- Make sure you back up the changed version.

- For important spreadsheets consider keeping a log of the changes you make. Include date, reason and nature of change made.

- Check all the changes that you make.

If there are links from your spreadsheet to other spreadsheets or applications which are owned by different people, before making changes contact the people who link to your spreadsheet so that they are aware of the changes.

 DOCUMENTING YOUR SPREADSHEET

Many people consider documenting a spreadsheet to be overkill – only for large, centrally managed systems. However, just because a spreadsheet is produced and maintained in an 'end-user' environment does not mean its details should not be written down. **Good documentation can help those who have to maintain the spreadsheet as well as those who use it**.

If your spreadsheet uses information from another source, make sure that details are included in the documentation associated with the source. If, for example, your spreadsheet uses values from another spreadsheet, details about the other one should be included in yours and in the other (source) spreadsheet.

Although separate documentation can be helpful, there are usually some facilities for building documentation into the spreadsheet itself. For example you can use labels, notes, titles and instructions to guide users. You can note down the worksheet title, subject, author and other details within the spreadsheet file. (*How*: From the Menu toolbar choose File, Properties and select the Summary tab. Also select the Contents tab to enter the contents of each sheet of a workbook.)

For important spreadsheets consider making a back-up of any documentation which is not a part of the spreadsheet itself.

KEYPOINTS

✔ Keep your spreadsheets up-to-date, and secure.

✔ Make sure your spreadsheets are accessible to the people who read them.

✔ Consider password-protecting the spreadsheets and take steps to control changes to them.

✔ Include good documentation – it will help the spreadsheets' users and also help the people who have to maintain the spreadsheets.